Marlowe R. Scott

ABIDING
is not
HIDING

Safe in His Arms

Marlowe R. Scott

Pearly Gates Publishing LLC
INSPIRING CHRISTIAN AUTHORS TO BE AUTHORS

Pearly Gates Publishing, LLC, Houston, Texas (USA)

Abiding is not Hiding

Abiding is Not Hiding:
Safe in His Arms

Copyright © 2020
Marlowe R. Scott

All Rights Reserved.
No portion of this publication may be reproduced, stored in an electronic system, or transmitted in any form or by any means (electronic, mechanical, photocopy, recording, or otherwise) without written permission from the author or publisher. Brief quotations may be used in literary reviews.

Print ISBN 13: 978-1-947445-79-6
Digital ISBN 13: 978-1-947445-80-2
Library of Congress Control Number: 2020901198

Scripture references are taken from the King James Version (KJV) of the Holy Bible and used with permission via Zondervan. Public Domain.

For information and bulk ordering, contact:
Pearly Gates Publishing, LLC
Angela Edwards, CEO
P.O. Box 62287
Houston, TX 77205
BestSeller@PearlyGatesPublishing.com

Marlowe R. Scott

Dedication

To my Mother,

Helena R. Winrow-Harris
(1918 – 1992):

A woman who was blessed with many talents.

Acknowledgments

Thanking God for accepting me into His Christian family through His Son, my Savior Jesus Christ.

Praising and forever grateful for the blessings received by being a mother myself. The scriptures say that children are a gift from God, and I have seen my gifts become strong and productive children who know Jesus Christ for themselves.

Words cannot express the gifts manifested through my daughter, **Angela R. Edwards**. She has developed into a glowing example of sharing God's love and messages through Pearly Gates Publishing, LLC, and Redemption's Story Publishing, LLC, of which she is the CEO. Countless men's and women's, as well as youth's lives, have been enriched and changed by the publishing of their stories through her publishing houses.

Last, but not least, I thank my husband, **Andrew Scott**, for patiently giving me quiet time and space to write my books. This adds blessings and luxuries to my creative spirit.

Marlowe R. Scott

Preface

As God would have it, I became inspired to write this book by something unexpected. The date was December 20, 2019. I had taken an online character assessment that stated the word for me for 2020 was **"ABIDE."**

I searched for the meaning of 'abide' and found that the definition definitely pertained to me—especially at this stage of my life! I strive for patience, accept things that are true in accordance with a rule or decision, have withstood several trials, and am tolerant in trying circumstances with others.

Almost immediately after that revelation, a familiar song from my Methodist upbringing flooded my memory: "Abide with Me" by Henry Francis Lyle (initially authored in 1847). More about that hymn is shared within my story. There are direct quotes attributed to Jesus Christ concerning "abiding in Him."

As the messages in *Abiding is Not Hiding: Safe in His Arms* are read and, prayerfully, understood, it is my sincerest prayer and desire that you soak in the blessings. There is no better place to be than in the safety of the loving arms of Jesus Christ!

Marlowe R. Scott

Introduction

THEME TEXT: John 15:4-5

"Abide in Me, and I in you. As the branch cannot bear fruit of itself, except it abide in the vine; no more can ye, except ye abide in Me. I am the True Vine, ye are the branches: He that abideth in Me, and I in him, the same bringeth forth much fruit: for without Me, ye can do nothing."

In thinking about an example of abiding and being held safe in one's arms here on earth, I thought about new parents holding, cuddling, rocking, and singing to their infant. The scene is beautiful, peaceful, and loving. The anticipated new life has come, bringing with it all of its wonders.

Now, let's imagine a loving Jesus Christ, waiting for us to be born again into His family. His arms are eagerly waiting to receive us, save our souls, and love us. As a part of Jesus' family, we are attached (so to speak) to the **TRUE VINE** found in John 15:1 — *"I am the **TRUE VINE**, and My Father is the Husbandman"* (emphasis added). **(Those are the words spoken by Jesus Christ. Those with a Holy**

Bible with Jesus' words in red type will easily see whenever He speaks in the New Testament.) It was customary for Jesus to use plants and nature to make His illustrations clear to those hearing Him. That is evident in the numerous parables He spoke.

The plant life used for the writing of this book (for illustrative purposes) is the familiar grapevine. It is interesting to know that grapes, grapevines, winepresses, and wines are mentioned more than any plant source throughout the entirety of the Holy Bible. Even the mention of vinegar was commonly associated with grapes as its source.

As the messages given to me are shared on the pages of this book, there is a chapter on grapevines that will demonstrate characteristics reflective of how we are connected to Jesus, *"The TRUE VINE,"* as stated in John 15:1.

To you, Dear Reader, I say:

Enjoy! Be blessed and nourished as you draw ever closer to Jesus Christ!

Marlowe R. Scott

Table of Contents

DEDICATION .... **VI**

ACKNOWLEDGMENTS .... **VII**

PREFACE .... **VIII**

INTRODUCTION .... **X**

CHAPTER ONE 1

    ABIDE'S ASSURANCE

CHAPTER TWO 4

    HYMNS ARE TIMELESS

CHAPTER THREE 16

    NOWHERE TO HIDE

CHAPTER FOUR 21

    THE BLESSINGS OF GOD'S GRACE

CHAPTER FIVE 24

    VINE CONNECTIONS

ABIDING IS NOT HIDING 28

    A POEM BY MARLOWE R. SCOTT © 2020

CHAPTER SIX 29

    THE TRUE VINE

CONCLUSION 31

CLOSING PRAYER 35

ABOUT THE AUTHOR 36

BEST-SELLING BOOKS BY MARLOWE R. SCOTT 39

CONTACT MARLOWE R. SCOTT 47

Marlowe R. Scott

Chapter One

Abide's Assurance

Hymns can be mini-sermons at times. The messages I often receive spark many memories. Each verse of the hymn, *"Abide with Me,"* gives me peace, assurance, and hope. Although Henry Francis Lyte wrote it in 1847, the hymn gives me insights into the stages of life while always confirming that we need the Lord Jesus Christ to always abide with us.

So, exactly what does "abide" and "abideth" mean? I am so glad you asked!

Definitions of abide are:

- ❖ To accept without objection;
- ❖ To act in accordance with a rule, decision, or recommendation;
- ❖ Bear patiently;
- ❖ Tolerate;
- ❖ Endure without yielding; and
- ❖ To wait for.

Abide is used over 80 times in scriptures, and abideth is used approximately 30 times.

Disappointingly, neither word is used often in today's highly technological world. While the word abideth may be categorized as an archaic verb, I truly believe it is still relevant. Jesus was definitely not using archaic wording; rather, He used meaningful and unchanging words when He spoke. They are in the Holy Scriptures, serve a purpose, and have meaning.

The word "ABIDE" is a verb, meaning there is action involved. It is found in the Old Testament in

Psalm 91:1 — *"He that dwelleth in the secret place of the Most High shall **ABIDE** under the shadow of the Almighty"* (emphasis added). It is also found in 1 Corinthians 3:14 — *"If any man's work **ABIDE** which he hath built thereupon, he shall receive a reward"* (emphasis added).

A sampling of scriptures that mention the word "abideth" include:

John 8:35 — *"And the servant **ABIDETH** not in the house for ever: but the Son **ABIDETH** ever"* (emphasis added).

1 Peter 1:23 — *"Being born again, not of corruptible seed, but of incorruptible, by the Word of God, which liveth and **ABIDETH** forever"* (emphasis added).

Chapter Two

Hymns Are Timeless

As shared earlier, many hymns—some written millenniums ago—inspire me and help me along my Christian journey. Many churches today do not use hymns regularly, but the influence of those inspired messages was destined to last for many years. God's messages through His hymn composers are timeless.

I previously mentioned the hymn *"Abide with Me,"* and have included the verses in this writing. After each verse, I have shared a few thoughts about what the words mean to me. After my personal comments, you are encouraged to write how you were touched and inspired by each verse.

****

LITTLE-KNOWN FACT:

In researching Hymnary.org, there is a list of 86 books including hymnals, worship and praise publications, as well as general song books containing the inspiring *"Abide with Me"*.

Marlowe R. Scott

"ABIDE WITH ME"

Verse 1:
"Abide with me: fast falls the eventide; the darkness deepens, LORD, with me abide. When other helpers fail, and comforts flee, Help of the helpless, O abide with me."

Thoughts:

Sometimes, when we feel lonely or frustrated with circumstances, we take things into our own hands and try working them out ourselves. The opening words to this hymn are a simple plea for help/comfort when the walls seem to be closing in on us. Reaching out to friends, family, and others offer no help when impatience and peace are gone. Only then do the words come to plead, *"O abide with me."*

Abiding is not Hiding

Describe how you are inspired by the verse.

Verse 2:

"Swift to its close ebbs out life's little day; earth's joys grow dim, its glories pass away. Change and decay in all around I see. O thou who changest not, abide with me."

Thoughts:

Circumstances that used to cause joy, happiness, and former fond feelings are absent. Life seems to decay (fall apart) and be in a state of dreariness and death-like. Yet again, the unchanging Helper—Jesus—comes, and we plead, *"Abide with me."*

Abiding is not Hiding

Describe how you are inspired by the verse.

Verse 3:

"I need Thy presence every passing hour. What but Thy grace, can foil the tempter's power? Who like Thyself my guide and strength can be? Through cloud and sunshine, O abide with me."

Thoughts:

Our soul admits the need of our God every passing hour. We remember that God's grace guards us against the influence and temptations of Satan. Through it all, we recognize that God is stronger than that fallen angel (Satan), and we plead, *"Abide with me."*

Abiding is not Hiding

Describe how you are inspired by the verse.

Verse 4:
"I fear no foe with Thee at hand to bless, ills have no weight, and tears no bitterness. Where is death's sting? Where, grave, thy victory? I triumph still, if Thou abide with me."

Thoughts:

Now that I am reminded that with God always abiding with me and Satan's power is ineffective, I am confident that no foe coming against me needs to be feared. The heaviness of sickness does not weigh my spirit down. The bitterness of falling tears ceases. I consider and ask myself, *"Where is the sting of death?"* or *"Where is the victory of the grave?"* I know I am a winner and overcomer because of the assurance that Heaven is my promised triumphant goal when God and my savior Jesus Christ abide with me.

Abiding is not Hiding

Describe how you are inspired by the verse.

Verse 5:
"Hold thou thy cross before my closing eyes. Shine through the gloom and point me to the skies. Heaven's morning breaks and earth's vain shadows flee; in life, in death, O Lord abide with me."

Thoughts:

As my earthly body is nearing death, the Cross of Jesus I'll long to see. The Cross shines through the gloom all around me and points my soul toward Heaven. Once there, the brightness of glory explodes, and the earth's memories swiftly flee away. I begin shouting and praising God, saying, *"In life and in death,* **THANK YOU, LORD, FOR ABIDING WITH ME!"**

Abiding is not Hiding

Describe how you are inspired by the verse.

Marlowe R. Scott

Chapter Three

Nowhere to Hide

The title of this book uses the word "HIDING." Why? The answer is simple yet complicated for some:

No one can hide from God, no matter how hard they try! *That's a fact!*

Again, let's look at some scriptures:

Jeremiah 23:24 — *"'Can any hide himself in secret places that I shall not see him?' saith the LORD. 'Do I not fill Heaven and earth?' saith the LORD."*

Hebrews 4:13 — *"Neither is there any creature that is not manifest in His sight; but all things are naked and opened unto the eyes of Him with whom we have to do."*

There are familiar bible stories of instances where someone tried to hide, but God had other plans.

One is Joseph's story, as told in Genesis 37. Joseph was initially cast into a well by his brothers to die because they were jealous of him. Hiding him did not work because God intervened, and Joseph ended up being sold as a slave in Egypt. He eventually found favor and was raised to power. God had given him a gift of dreams and interpretation. In time, a dream he had told his brothers about of them bowing down to him came true. They were forced to seek help when a great famine came. In Egypt they bowed down to Joseph but did not recognize him. They were forgiven. As Joseph was in a position to help his brothers and aging father, he supplied not only food, but also comfortable lodging for his family.

Another is Moses' story, as found in Exodus 2. He is well-known for leading God's people out of captivity in Egypt, but as an infant, he was hidden in a basket to be saved from a decree to kill all the male babies of his heritage. God did it again! Moses was found in that basket and raised as an Egyptian, not knowing his true background. He rose to be a leader, but one day killed an Egyptian then buried the body in the sand. Eventually, Pharaoh found out about the incident and sought to have Moses killed. Moses escaped and fled to Midian.

David was said to have been "a man after God's own heart." His story is found in the Book of 2 Samuel. The sin he committed was giving into lustful desires with Bathsheba who was Uriah's wife. The sin was revealed when it was discovered that Bathsheba became pregnant because David gave into his lust while Uriah was at war. The sin David tried to **HIDE** was the pregnancy—the result of being intimate with Bathsheba. In an effort to hide his sin David had Uriah placed in the front of a battle which assured the certain death of Uriah. After Uriah's death, David married Bathsheba, but the conceived child died. In time, David and Bathsheba were blessed by God with another child, Solomon, who rose to become a wise and powerful king!

The Book of Jonah has been made into movies and is included in many children's books. God had told Jonah to go to Ninevah with a prophecy God gave him to save the people from destruction. Jonah rebelled and tried to hide from God's directions. He ended up being swallowed by a great fish and remained there until he was spat out of the fish's mouth onto dry land. Only then did Jonah finally obey God, going to Ninevah to give the word God told him.

Not to be left out, our Savior Jesus Christ also had instances when God protected Him, beginning when He was an infant. For protection from being harmed by Herod, Jesus' parents (Joseph and Mary) had been told by the Three Wise Men that Herod wanted to see the infant. Herod's intention was to harm the baby Jesus. An angel appeared to Joseph and told them to flee to Egypt for protection. This story is found in Matthew 2.

There are other stories within The Gospels where Jesus appeared to men and events as an adult, and then disappeared out of sight.

Chapter Four

The Blessings of God's Grace

Another familiar hymn I love is by John Newton written in 1779. The title is *"Amazing Grace"*! It is often heard at funerals by various Christian denominations, movies, ceremonies, and theatrical presentations—just to name a few. *"Amazing Grace"* tells a story about being found or saved by Jesus. The verses speak of life's emotional and spiritual journey until finally being called by God to our heavenly home.

The instances of hiding mentioned previously, are a form receiving God's grace which is truly amazing! Grace is given to His children through Jesus Christ. It enables us to have power and spiritual healing through the mercy and love of Jesus Christ. Grace gives us the strength to endure trials and resist temptation. It is God's favor and help in times of trouble.

God does not provide us with **EVERYTHING** we want and desire. We must remember that things happen according to God's will and timing. Be assured of this one thing: He will complete the work begun in us as we grow in Jesus Christ. We will have restoration of peace, joy, and rewards beyond measure – *"Joy, Unspeakable Joy,"* as some Christians have been heard saying.

NOTE: Over the years, other versions of "Amazing Grace" may have adopted different words. However, the central message basically remains the same.

AMAZING GRACE

Verse 1:
"Amazing grace, how sweet the sound, that saved a wretch like me! I once was lost, but now am found; was blind, but now I see."

Verse 2:
"'Twas grace that taught my heart to fear, and grace my fears relieved. How precious did that grace appear the hour I first believed!"

Verse 3:
"Through many dangers, toils, and snares, I have already come: 'Tis grace has brought me safe thus far, and grace will lead me home."

Verse 4:
"The Lord has promised good to me, His Word my hope secures; He will my shield and portion be, as long as life endures."

Verse 5:
"Yes, when this flesh and heart shall fail, and mortal life shall cease; I shall possess, within the veil, a life of joy and peace."

Verse 6:
"The earth shall soon dissolve like snow, the sun forbears to shine; but God, who called me here below, will be forever mine."

Chapter Five

Vine Connections

What does a grapevine (or any other vine) have to do with being connected to and protected in the arms of Jesus Christ?

Before sharing further information and analogies, consider the following as found in 1 Corinthians 1:27 —

"But God hath chosen the foolish things of the world to confound the wise; and God hath chosen the weak things of the world to confound the things which are mighty..."

"Confound" is interpreted as to confuse, perplex, amaze, and bewilder.

For those who have read that Jesus is the **TRUE VINE** (John 15), we may not fully understand why a vine was used. Remember that Jesus used things of nature and even farming examples in His many parables and illustrations. It is easy to use the grapevine, although scriptures do not say explicitly that the vine illustrations were grapevines.

However, it must be noted that grapevines are strong, provide nourishment, are a source of protection, and more. A shortlist of other fruit-bearing vines is:

- Blackberries
- Raspberries
- Kiwi
- Some strawberries

My personal knowledge of the grapevine and brief study shows that the vine grows rapidly from a well-rooted trunk. From this trunk, canes develop and attach to trees, trellises, and other things. For grape farmers, they usually use wire for the canes to connect to. If you are like me, you have also seen many tendrils reaching out as more support. Then, pretty-shaped leaves develop and, in time, the grape clusters.

Considering how the vines are always reaching out and grasping a hold onto something, they are perfect for thinking of the arms of Jesus Christ. He is always reaching and holding onto those who come to Him as a member of the Christian family! When in His arms, we find so much love, peace, and protection. When the winds and storms of life come, they shake us, but He does not let go.

Something that may not be easy for Christians to understand is that, at times, the "attachment" may experience a 'pruning process.' Why? Because pruning cuts away old habits, former weaknesses, old familiar friends, etc. The pruning allows for and encourages new growth for the grapevine and, more importantly, **US!**

In times past, I have cut back the wild grapevines in my yard, yet the tendrils refused to drop to the ground—although they were clearly cut off. Can you relate? We find ourselves still holding on, even though that "thing" we were so attached to can no longer support or help us. Eventually, the pruned tendrils die, but not without first swinging about with no place to go.

Marlowe R. Scott

Abiding is Not Hiding
A Poem by Marlowe R. Scott © 2020

As a child I played a game;
It was called Hide and Seek.
One person would try to find me,
As I hid somewhere and peeked.
Should that person get close,
I'd move further out of their view;
Behind a bush or house corner,
Until I could run before getting tagged
And hear the words "*I got you!*"
As I have aged, looked back, and seen
Many times, I played the game, Hide and Seek,
With my Savior Jesus
Who died on Calvary for me.
I now know in Jesus, there is no hiding;
He knows everything I have done.
Jesus knows my reckless and thoughtless times,
Times when falling short of his demands.
Then, when I repent and confess my shortcomings,
Pleading for forgiveness,
His arms are always outstretched;
Open to receive me
Because He has loved me through it all!
The joy, peace, and LOVE I receive
Flood the depths of my soul.
His forgiveness is mine once again,
As in the safety of His arms I rest,
Basking in His Mercy, Grace, and Glory I cling!

Chapter Six

The TRUE VINE

For those who have found safety and comfort in the arms of Jesus, I share the following passages of scripture with you. At the right time, may they will provide comfort and assurance.

Rejoice at all times – Philippians 4:4
"Rejoice in the LORD alway; and again, I say, Rejoice!"

Be content – Philippians 4:11
"Not that I speak in respect of want: for I have learned, in whatever state I am, therewith to be content."

Be strengthened – Philippians 4:13
"I can do all things through Christ, which strengtheneth me."

Needs supplied – Philippians 4:19
"But my God shall supply all your need according to His riches in glory by Christ Jesus."

The simplistic explanation is that by being attached to the **TRUE VINE**—Jesus Christ—we have help and clarity in decision-making and knowing the right way to go. Our minds (formerly influenced by Satan) and the world are changed. We become convicted when we are tempted to stray!

An exciting aspect for me is that being attached to the **TRUE VINE** has helped me grow in the Fruit of the Spirit found in Galatians 5: **Love, Joy, Peace, Patience, Kindness, Goodness, Faithfulness, Gentleness, and Self-Control!**

Conclusion

Should the title, *Abiding is Not Hiding: Safe in His Arms,* sounds odd when you first saw it, prayerfully, by reading and thinking about the scriptures, hymns, and examples given, you have gained an understanding of the intention of the message in its entirety.

Scripture clearly states that Jesus Christ is the **TRUE VINE** for Christians — those who have acknowledged we are born into a sinful world. Our Creator (God) had to give us a way to get back to Him, so He sent His Son Jesus Christ! Acknowledging that being connected to the **TRUE VINE** does not guarantee us a carefree and blissful life. However, being connected does give security and support by the outstretched arms of Jesus Christ, which holds back utter destruction of our lives. As scriptures, some hymnals and spirituals share, our trials come to make us strong. Jesus Christ will go with us through the troubled waters of this life.

The five examples of instances when scriptures shared times when well-known characters were in hiding or hidden by others. Each ended up in a God-directed place far from where the situation that caused the hiding began. The 'world' has a simple and true statement saying:

"You can run, but you cannot hide!"

QUESTION: *If people in general know this, why try to hide from God and Jesus Christ?*

Joseph's brothers planned to get rid of him because of jealousy. God's plan was different. Joseph was sold into slavery, interpreted dreams, gained favor with people, ended up a leader, and, in time of famine, was able to save his brothers and father.

Moses was saved from a basket his mother hid him in. He was rescued by Pharaoh's daughter and treated like royalty. After killing an Egyptian, he fled to Midian. He later returned to Egypt and freed the Israelites from bondage.

David lusted after Bathsheba and had her husband put in a situation to be killed in battle to hide the fact that Bathsheba was pregnant by David. The child died, but God later blessed David to be the father of Solomon, who would become a wise king.

Jonah was told to go to Ninevah to tell them to change their ways or be destroyed. He went to hide and ended up being swallowed by a great fish. Jonah was in the fish's belly for three days and prayed all the while. The fish spit him out, and Jonah finally went to Ninevah to give God's message to the people.

Jesus Christ was hidden as an infant by his earthly parents after the three wise men told them about Herod wanting to see the baby because he understood a **KING** had been born. An angel told the family to flee to Egypt for safety. Herod didn't know about the promise of the coming *KING JESUS, THE KING OF KINGS!*

With each of the unusual occurrences, God's protection and devine guidance were manifested. **PRAISE THE LORD!**

A PERSONAL INVITATION: Should anyone reading this book feel the presence of Jesus calling you into His family, I encourage you to choose to join us *NOW*.

For those who have gleaned something new and are strengthened, my prayer is that the growth continues for you and those whom you touch.

To everyone, consider this: Without the abiding, constant presence of the **TRUE VINE**, Jesus Christ, we could do *NOTHING* of eternal value.

Finally, the greatest blessing is when the resurrected Jesus Christ welcomes our souls in our eternal heavenly home!

Closing Prayer

*Lord and Savior Jesus Christ,
May the words of this book give blessings and increase territories of those who serve you —*
THE TRUE VINE.

AMEN

About the Author

Marlowe R. Scott [Harris] was born at home in a small farming community located in Cedarville, New Jersey. Her parents are the late Carl and Helena Harris [Winrow]. Marlowe is a true country girl who loves nature — God's wondrous creation. She enjoys seeing birds preparing nests, wild turkeys roaming the backyard with their young, and the stately deer in the field and property tree line where she lives in Browns Mills, New Jersey.

Marlowe has been blessed with many talents. They include writing, poetry, music, sewing, crocheting, quilting, and floral designs. Her educational focus was the Communication Arts Degree Program at Burlington County College, as well as attendance and participation in numerous government-sponsored training venues.

Marlowe's extensive experiences encompassed duties as: Leadership, Education, and Development Facilitator; Equal Employment Opportunity Counselor; Quality Management Facilitator; and member of the New Jersey Quality Board of Examiners. With her commitment to quality, she also participated in videoconferences, workshops, and community volunteer activities.

One highlight of her career was a conference held in Baltimore, Maryland where she was a member of a select group of individuals who met and interacted with Retired U.S. Army General and Former U.S. Secretary of State, Colin Powell. Marlowe retired after 33 years of dedicated federal civil service.

She has taught Floral Arts and Crafts in adult education, won ribbons for her creative designs, and appeared on television and in newspapers. Currently, she devotes much of her time to quilting and developing her home-based business, M.R.S. Inspirations, with the motto "Magnificent Revelations Are My Specialty." Her creations are focused on making special memories in lap quilts, throws, baby quilts, and pillows which show love and give comfort to the recipient.

Readers of Marlowe's books have verbally expressed, as well as given written endorsements and testimonies, sharing how they were inspired, experienced spiritual growth, and were comforted through her writings and poems. She also received commendation from Former U.S. President Barack Obama and family for sharing with them her first piece of literary art, *Spiritual Growth: From Milk to Strong Meat*.

Marlowe is married to Andrew Scott and has three children: Carl, James, and Angela, as well as five grandchildren and a host of great-grandchildren. She is currently a member of Tabernacle Baptist Church in Burlington, New Jersey.

Best-Selling Books by Marlowe R. Scott

Spiritual Growth: From Milk to Strong Meat
© 2015
www.amazon.com/Spiritual-Growth-Milk-Strong-Meat/dp/1511777702

Believing Without Seeing: The Power of Faith
© 2015
www.amazon.com/Believing-Without-Seeing-Power-Faith/dp/1515321258

Keeping It Real: The Straight and Narrow
© 2016
www.amazon.com/Keeping-Real-Straight-Marlowe-Scott/dp/1945117125

Marlowe R. Scott

Worth the Journey: The Train Ride to Glory
© 2016
www.amazon.com/Worth-Journey-Train-Ride-Glory/dp/1945117478

Abiding is not Hiding

Never Alone: Intimate Times with Jesus
© 2017
www.amazon.com/Never-Alone-Intimate-Times-Jesus/dp/1945117796

Marlowe R. Scott

"I AM" Cares: His Eyes Are on the Sparrow
© 2018
www.amazon.com/AM-Cares-His-Eye-Sparrow/dp/1947445162

Abiding is not Hiding

Plentiful Harvest: Fertile Ground
© 2018
www.amazon.com/Plentiful-Harvest-Fertile-Marlowe-Scott/dp/1947445375

Marlowe R. Scott

Talli's Ancestry Surprise: Beginning the Ancestral Search
© 2019
www.amazon.com/Tallis-Ancestry-Surprise-Beginning-Ancestral/dp/1947445588

Abiding is not Hiding

Contact Marlowe R. Scott

Marlowe R. Scott
Owner/Creator

Text: (609) 202-0535
Email: **m.r.boyce@att.net**
Browns Mills, NJ

"Specializing in Hand-Crafted Creations Giving Special Comfort and LOVE"

- ❖ Memory Pillows
- ❖ Memory Quilts
- ❖ Crib Quilts
- ❖ Throws
- ❖ And much, much more!

Marlowe R. Scott

www.ingramcontent.com/pod-product-compliance
Lightning Source LLC
Chambersburg PA
CBHW052124110526
44592CB00013B/1739